BORN HAUNTED

MY LIFELONG ENCOUNTERS WITH THE PARANORMAL

NATE MICHAEL

The official *Born Haunted* website:

https://www.bornhaunted.com

To contact the author, please write:

author@bornhaunted.com

For media relations , please write:

media@bornhaunted.com

For sales inquiries, please write:

sales@bornhaunted.com   or   https://www.bornhaunted.com

TABLE OF CONTENTS

DEDICATION

The following pages are dedicated to the individuals currently being affected by paranormal activity. I am referring to those that feel scared and helpless in their own homes. Our homes are supposed to be a sanctuary, a place we can come back to at the end of a busy day. I too have suffered from those same feelings that make your home uninhabitable. On several different occasions, in fact.

Everyone will have a paranormal experience at least once in their life. However, experiencing paranormal activity often goes unreported, and folks attempt to "explain away" their encounter. Many don't even realize what they experienced was out of the ordinary. Sometimes, a paranormal event cannot be explained away. Sometimes, the evidence is too blatant to blame on the wind or old creaky floorboards. Sometimes the paranormal evidence is so irrefutable that it turns skeptics into believers. And unfortunately, it sometimes causes psychological and mental strain on individuals and their families.

Living in an environment affected by paranormal activity draws out a primal fear in an individual. And if that's not bad enough, the fear of confiding in others that your "home is haunted", is just as horrifying. The fear of being labeled "crazy" by your peers is just as primal.

For those who are experiencing paranormal events, and feel they have no one to turn to, no one to talk to about the subject, this book is for you. I am here for you. I invite you to re-read this dedication should you feel afraid due to the paranormal. There is also a section in this book featuring some advice on living with the paranormal. And if that is not enough, I invite you to reach out to me and I would be happy to lend a listening ear, and provide any advice on the topic I have gathered throughout the years.

Ghosts, spirits, hauntings, or whatever you wish to call them, are very real. The paranormal is very real. And honestly, contrary to what you may think, the paranormal is a very *normal* thing.

You are not alone, my friend. I encourage you to not live in fear, but to open your mind and accept those things which science cannot explain. Live happily in knowledge.

- Nate Michael -

And to the love of my life:

Thank you for being by my side, helping me and supporting me, no matter what. This book is also dedicated to you because you didn't know what the hell you were getting into when you said "Yes!" to marrying me. I love you.

INTRODUCTION

I have always felt I live a normal life. I work, I watch TV, and I like a cold beer. I apologize in advance, as I tend to cuss a lot. I'm slightly overweight. My point is, I'm completely the average guy. If you were to walk past me on the street, nothing screams "this guy has a plethora of paranormal experiences and knowledge". Although I'm open to publicly discussing my encounters with the paranormal, I generally refrain from initiating the topic. However, if the topic is raised among open minded people, I am sure to share my experience and knowledge.

To be honest, many acquaintances of mine would never even know I have directly been affected by ghostly or paranormal activity. Some of these acquaintances (several being paranormal skeptics), would scoff at you if you told them that I've experienced the supernatural, the paranormal, throughout my life. Some would even say, "No, not him! He's not out of his damn mind!" And I'm not out of my damn mind. I'm a normal, healthy individual, with a hell-of-a-lot of very true and personal ghost stories to tell.

I began my professional career in healthcare as a nurse assistant. I would provide basic patient care to individuals at a nursing home. I quickly rose in the ranks and was asked to continue my education so I could perform more medical procedures like wound treatment, medication administration, and other duties at the nursing facility.

It wasn't long after completing further education that I quickly joined the management/administrative team at the nursing home. After working for that particular company for nearly seven years, I decided I wanted to achieve my goal and dream of working at a large and fast-paced hospital. I was quickly welcomed to one of my home region's county hospitals. I specifically worked in the Intensive Care Unit, and absolutely loved the position! The ICU was very fast-paced, and much like its name, it was intense! There was much to learn about the hospital, and there were many differences from the nursing home. There were also many similarities.

Unfortunately, one of those similarities is the fact of death. Death is no stranger to the medical community, and visited both the hospital and the nursing home (I would venture to say that death visited the nursing home a little more regularly, though). One could say that in healthcare, death is a fact of life. It is a part of the job.

On several occasions, I was given the task of providing medication, patient care, and being present at the bedside while a patient was experiencing the death process. It was never an easy job to do. Witnessing a patient, a person- someone's mother or father- gasp as they draw their final breath, is always an extremely emotional event. No matter how often or routinely it occurred.

As my experience and years in healthcare grew, I became more comfortable with the frequency of death. It was no longer as intimidating to see and care for those patients entering their end of life stage. I began to correlate aspects of different patients' end of life processes, and noticed striking similarities.

Shortly before someone begins the dying process, they often claim hallucinations of loved ones long deceased. They would state seeing their husband or wife floating above their bed. A husband or wife that had passed away many years ago. And those whom still had some minor vocal ability as they were actively dying, often would whisper things about a bright white light at the end of a tunnel.

Though my childhood did not consist of much church-going, my siblings and I were taught modern Christian teachings. We attended non-denominational Christian church on holidays, and attended some Bible school events as young children. It wasn't until my teenage years that my natural curiosity (inner rebelliousness, and Scorpio zodiac sign) led me to begin reading about other schools of religion.

I became fascinated with the multitude of world religions I was discovering in books, and soaked up as much of the religious knowledge I could. I read materials on Buddhism, Judaism, Wicca and Witchcraft,

Paganism, Zoroastrianism, Hinduism, and everything in-between. I especially loved the religions of ancient Greece and Egypt. The ancient gods of the Inca and Maya always provided a fascinating read.

Parallel to my years experience in healthcare, my knowledge of world religions grew and I realized that I no longer identified solely as a non-denominational Christian. I renounced my practicing of the Christian faith shortly after a profound spiritual experience. An experience where I was shown the connection between birth and death. An experience where I was a direct witness to reincarnation. This experience, coupled with the large amount of paranormal occurrence in my childhood, led me to my current path of practicing the nature-loving and peaceful traditions of Wicca and Witchcraft.

The "light at the end of the tunnel" that I mentioned above, the light they saw, was real. And though they may have been dying, I believe they were also being re-birthed. This profound spiritual moment presented me with what happens after we die. It showed me what is in the afterlife. And it was all related to that tunnel with the light at the end. For me, it not only explains the afterlife; it explains many of the paranormal run-ins I have had throughout my existence.

Though, this writing is not regarding my religious philosophy, I feel it is important to briefly touch on. It is important because ghostly, paranormal activity occurs across nearly every religious ideology. Ghosts and the paranormal encompasses a huge section of the world's ancient, and even current religions. The Greeks, Romans, Egyptians, Sumerians, Mongolians, and Native American Indians all believed in some form of the paranormal. Oftentimes, those ideas and beliefs on the paranormal were nearly identical.

Though those ancient religions have long since passed on, ghosts have not. They are still here and active as ever. As science advances and old technologies fade to nostalgic memories, ghosts will not. They will continue to be as active as ever. Ghosts will never become a thing of the past. They will always be among us. The laws of physics state they will continue on to 'haunt' the living. "Physics!?", you might ask.

How can the laws of physics, the very laws of science and the natural world, prove the existence of ghosts? The most brief, simplest, and unarguably scientific way to answer that question is: The Law Of Conservation Of Energy. Energy is never created, and it is also never destroyed. It is said to be conserved over time; energy transforms from one form, to another.

What is living today, may be a ghost tomorrow.

CHAPTER ONE

Evil Spirits In The Closet

"Let's get back in bed, Dear," Mom said as she gathered my blankets, pillows, and plush stuffed animals. "Why do you want to sleep in the living room when you have a nice, comfy bed in your own room?"

Still upset from the noises, I answered, "I don't like my room, it's scary." This behavior was not new. It was becoming a nightly event to gather my sleeping items and catch a few hours of rest on the couch. As the sun stretched upwards across the horizon, Mom or Dad would carry me back to my room, gently placing me in bed. They were careful not to wake me.

The nightly battle of keeping me in my bed was taking its toll. So much so, they even made an appointment with my pediatrician.

"He absolutely will not stay in his room," my parents told the doctor.

"He says it's too scary," Mom added.

"And literally cries so hard, he pukes all over himself," Dad chimed in.

There was nothing medically wrong, though. I was a normal, healthy kid. Doc chalked it up to a common childhood fear of the dark. He prescribed nothing more than a night-light, a stuffed animal or *blankie*, and a cold-hard dose of parental love.

"Calmly clean him up if he vomits, and put him back in bed. Shut the door if he cries too loud; he needs to learn to sleep in his own room," the doctor advised.

And so, night after night, my parents would do just that. After I discovered the pattern of them trying to calm me down, their refusal to let me out of my room, and then the dreaded closed door- I began making my way to the couch. It was better there, than in my room with that terrifying closet.

The sounds coming from that closet would scare the piss out of me. I would literally urinate on my potty-trained self. It wasn't just creaks or moans from an old floorboard. It was much, much more than that. I often wonder if that closet is the root cause of the insomnia issues I still struggle with today.

It wasn't just the audible whispers from the closet that gave me the skin-crawling feeling of fear. It was the fact that in those whispers I could hear my name. Someone talking to me. Or, about me. Whispering for me to "come in and play".

And then, when I was in tears crying for Mom through my bedroom door, the closet would ever-so-slightly open and the shadow would snake its way out; slithering across the floor like a serpent.

I would tell my parents about it, almost nightly. The noises. The whispers. The shadow. Every parent will experience a time when their child is afraid, for whatever reasoning, and won't sleep in their room. Most times, parents will blame these fears and experiences on their child's imagination.

Children's imaginations can often get carried away. A tree branch blowing in the wind can easily resemble a figure standing outside their bedroom window. It happens, it is normal. Children have very active imaginations, hence why parents tend to overlook their fears of the unknown.

Like most parents, mine alluded my fears to my imagination; one they thought I would outgrow. But, other strange events were soon to occur that couldn't be easily written-off to "the wind".

What I was experiencing was no imagination. It wasn't the ideas brought to life by a lonely kid who tried to entertain himself. Since it was the 1980s, it certainly could not have been something I viewed on any laptop, tablet, or internet device. Those pieces of technology weren't invented yet. I was too young to read or watch horror stories that would make me replicate them in my bedroom at night.

There would be little explanation for how I would soon begin to label what was in my closet, scaring me. The name I gave it, at a very young age, would make any parent's spine tingle. I described the shadow and whispers to my parents on many occasions; but one particular evening, I told them exactly what it was. Crying, and shaking in fear, I bolted from my room. I threw open the door and ran down the hall sobbing. Mom and Dad's bedroom door quickly flung open.

"What's wrong, Bud?" Dad asked. Mom jumped out of bed to comfort me. I was incoherently shouting while crying about the shadow, the whispers, and my closet.

"C'mon, Bud," Dad said. "It's late. Let's get back in bed."

I quickly interjected, "I can't sleep in there!"

"What's the matter this time?" Mom asked.

"The shadow in my closet, it came out and talked to me. It told me what it is," I said through tears.

"Okay…and who did it say it was, Bud?" they asked. Both of my parents' eyes widened, and jaws dropped as I replied,

"An evil spirit."

CHAPTER TWO

Welcome Home

Though continuing to remain skeptical, hearing their little boy tell them there was an evil spirit in his room, certainly made peculiar events not go unnoticed. Although I was quite young to understand what an evil spirit meant, I knew it was something sinister that caused me great fear and could hurt me.

The frequency of strange occurrences seemed to increase after the night I told them about my evil spirit roommate. So much so, my mom would soon have communication with the same entity.

After an afternoon of grocery shopping, and other errands, we arrived home in time for Mom to start prepping dinner. Just as the tires on our family car began crunching the gravel of our driveway, Mom let out a gasp.

"What the fuck?!" Dad shouted. The front door was wide open.

"Oh my God, Mike, look! The back door is open too!" Mom said to Dad.

"And I remember turning off the lights before we left," Mom pointed at the windows on our home.

"They are all on! Mike, someone's in there!" She shouted nervously, and in between gasps of air. Fiddling around at his waistline, Dad unsheathed the knife he kept on his belt for work.

"Go to the neighbors and ask to call the police. Stay in their yard, and don't go inside that damn house until the cops give the okay," Dad said in a calm, but very firm tone.

"GO! NOW, DAMMIT!" Dad shouted.

I began to sob. I was terrified of what was going on. Mom

grabbed my hand, and we ran towards the neighbors. I looked back to see my dad walking up the few steps leading into our (now open) front door. This made me cry harder. I could see the outline of Dad in the window blinds as he went from room to room, checking closets and peering underneath beds.

I prayed no one would jump out and hurt him. I prayed that he would be safe from the evil spirit when he opened my closet door.

"No robbers, Bud, just an evil fucking spirit," I imagined him saying. This was a funny thought to calm myself, as my mom was shouting into the neighbors phone about burglary and the possibility of someone hiding inside.

It wasn't long until law enforcement arrived. The two responding officers did a sweep of our house with guns drawn. The only thing they found was a normal looking home without anything out of place. Everything just as we left it. The small amount of money, stashed in an envelope on top of the refrigerator, remained untouched. Mom's little wooden jewelry box was sitting on her nightstand, locked, as it always ways. Nothing was missing and there was absolutely no sign of an intruder.

"Is it possible the door didn't latch on your way out, ma'am?" One of the officers asked.

"The door was shut. And locked," Mom said. "Even if it wasn't fully shut, how does that explain the backdoor being open?"

The other policeman responded, "Well, ma'am, if the door wasn't shut properly, that could create an air draft that makes other doors open; and who knows, maybe they just weren't fully latched."

"Hell, could've even been some teenage punks messing around, right?" The patrolman said, trying to be friendly.

"Or with the colder weather upon us, maybe it made the wood swell or something ma'am."

"But what about my freaking lights?!" Mom shouted at the officers.

"I clearly remember turning them off before we left; just like I remember shutting and locking the doors!" The explanations weren't making any sense to my mother who was convinced that something none of us could explain was going on. Realizing they weren't going to convince Mom otherwise, the two policemen turned to my dad.

"We'll file a report and send some officers to drive by on a regular basis tonight; if that sounds good with you."

"Sure. Sounds good, thanks," Dad replied with a confused expression. "I just don't get why they wouldn't take anything. And why nothing other than the lights on and the doors open, is out of place?" Dad asked as the officers got in their police cruiser.

"Rest assured folks, it was probably just the wind or something," one of them said as he entered the vehicle.

"If there's anything else you need this evening, feel free to give us a call. That's what the police are for," he said as he turned the ignition on the squad car.

It would be later that same night that Mom would have the urge to call the police again. This time, she could prove them wrong. However, she was going to quickly realize the police couldn't help us. The police only fight crime, they can't fight something they can't see. The cops can only arrest living bad guys, they can't arrest an evil spirit.

CHAPTER THREE

The Word In The Window

Even though the officers cleared the house of any would-be robbers, burglars, or bad guys, Mom and I were hesitant to go in. Dad, however, led the way.

"Can I play in the yard?" I asked. There was this heaviness in the house that frightened me and I wanted to be outdoors.

"Just until dinner is ready, and then we're locking the doors and staying in for the night! How about a movie later, Bud?" Mom asked, hoping a movie would keep her mind from wandering to all the strange, recent events.

"Yay! Movie, movie!" I chanted.

"Oh and stay in front of the window, where I can see you," Mom said as she reluctantly walked inside.

After dinner, everyone's nerves began to calm. I bathed and got into my pajamas. Mom popped us popcorn, and Dad washed his down with an ice cold beer. What was an eventful afternoon, was slowly turning into a normal night.

As the VHS tape reached its halfway mark, all of the good pieces of popcorn had been eaten. Only the crunchy kernels that stick in your teeth remained. Dad was working on his third beer. I was fighting to keep my eyes open.

When the weight of my eyelids grew too heavy to resist, I slipped into a deep sleep. Nightmares of the evil spirit in my closet played out in my dreams. I was dreaming that Mom was screaming for help. Several burglars in ski masks had a hold of Dad. There was a deep, dark laughter emanating from my closet. The police arrived, but the evil spirit in my closet came out and severed their heads clean off! There was nowhere to run, nowhere to hide, and no one to help. This made the spirit laugh even more. A sick and perverse laugh.

Mom decided I was resting peacefully, and she didn't want to wake me by putting me in my bed. The movie had ended a while ago, and Dad was trying to convince Mom to "take advantage of the alone time" (little did they know, this would result in my sister being born nine months later). I was fast asleep when they went to their bedroom.

Just before sunrise, Mom tossed the blankets back. She fiddled with her glasses before the time on the clock came into view. She glanced at her sleeping husband. He was snoring, uncovered, and wearing only a pair of whitey-tighties.

She was careful not to wake him as she tossed her legs over the edge of the bed; though, the thought did cross her mind. Images began reeling about the event that occurred with the lights and doors. She was too scared to stand from the bed. Too afraid to sit on the toilet by herself at such a late hour.

That was when she remembered I was still sleeping on the

couch. "Better tuck him in bed," she sighed as she stifled her uneasiness and grabbed her slippers. "And besides, I need to pee," she said aloud.

As she was finishing in the bathroom, washing her hands, she began to think about what the law enforcement officers said.

"Wood swelling," she muttered under her breath. Maybe the door's wooden casing did, in fact, swell; causing the door to not completely shut. Maybe they're right, she thought as she stared in the mirror, still washing her hands.

"We will send a patrolman to keep specific watch on this neighborhood, and your home tonight," Mom remembered an officer saying. This made her feel more at ease. She turned off the sink's tap and made her way out of the restroom. She glanced at her son, sleeping quietly on the couch.

She tossed around the idea of getting back under the toasty blankets, allowing me to finish up the night's rest on the sofa. It was nice to have one night of peace and quiet; "No evil spirits tonight,

Nate," she said to herself.

Just as she was beginning to turn around and head for the warm comfort of her bed, a horrible thought popped into her mind. She imagined three men in ski masks, quietly whispering outside our front door as they planned their crime. Her imaginative thoughts deepened and darkened as she visualized the men turning the knob on the front door. They quietly tip-toed into the living area. They spotted me slumbering away on the couch.

"Take the kid," one of the masked men whispered to the others. Mom shook her head, as if erasing the self-created, disturbing scenes from her thoughts. "Better just make sure it's locked," she mumbled. As she took her gaze off of me and to the front door, something caught her eye.

The narrow glass pane, on the top of the door, would normally peer into the cold darkness of a Midwestern fall night. Tonight, it drew Mom's attention. She began to slowly walk in its direction. She could tell something about the window on the front door wasn't normal.

Something wasn't right.

She peered over her shoulder to make sure I was still sleeping, then inched closer toward the door. A layer of condensation had formed on the interior side of the glass, and was blocking the meager view. It was a fog, like what is seen on a bathroom mirror after a long and hot shower. Her eyes darted, hoping to find a source for the mysterious condensation.

Her hair stood on end when she noticed writing; it resembled that when someone breathes their warm breath on a window or mirror, then uses their finger to draw or write. It wasn't a complete sentence that knocked the wind right out of her; It was a single word.

She screamed, "Mike, come out here and look at this!" I jumped from the couch, now wide awake. Mom was trembling in fear as she stared at that single word, legibly scrawled in the window's fog. It read: BITCH

My dad raced out of the room, holding a baseball bat. He

appeared crazy, and I know that if there had been a physical intruder, he was ready to defend his family. He calmed down when he saw that it was just us, my mom and I.

"What's happening?" Dad asked, Mom buried her head in his chest. Shaking, she pointed at the door's window. My father let go of her and went to the window, while my mother came to me; her arms enveloping me.

She was shaking terribly, and I could hear her heart pounding fast. She was really scared with what had just happened. This would be the first time I would see her shaken up so badly. This, however, wouldn't be the last.

My father was quiet. He kept staring at the lone written word on the window pane. Bitch.

"It could just be a coincidence," my father said. In the face of strange occurrences, we tend to blame such events on coincidence because we refuse to believe the possibility of otherwise. The door creaks, it is the wind. The light bulb goes off, it is a faulty wire. We humans have nonstop excuses to curb our fears.

Mom gave him a look. "A coincidence? Someone or *something* wrote that. Someone wrote it down for me to find." My father sighed, running his fingers through his hair, then he turned to me.

"Bud, did you see anything?" he asked. I drew closer to my mother whose arms tightened around me.

"I had nightmares. The spirit-" I whispered.

"Oh God! We shouldn't have left him out here. The writing is on the *inside* of the window; whoever or whatever did this was merely feet away from where our son was sleeping!" My mother's voice was consumed with panic. Her little boy had been alone in the living room with some form of intruder.

"Stay here, I will check around the house," my father said. While he went around the house, I told my mother my nightmare. I doubt she was listening, fixated on what she had just experienced.

"It's going to be okay," Mom said, ruffling my hair.

"The doors are locked, and we are the only ones in here. There's no way anyone can come in," Dad said. He looked at the window and as he repeated the statement, "It was just a coincidence." I knew even at a young age that he didn't believe in his words.

"We should go to bed now," he added.

"You're sleeping with us," Mom said, taking my hand. My father did not argue with her. We had all had an eventful day, and then, throw in the night. There was a sense of urgency to be together even if my father had checked the locks.

The three of us huddled together in the bed, with me between my parents. I could feel their rigid bodies, with tension, but eventually I fell asleep. This time around, there were no nightmares.

The following morning, the word on the window was gone. My mother had calmed down and she agreed with my father that last night had gotten to her. It has all been a coincidence. But I knew it hadn't been. The open doors, the lights turned on, and the bad word on the window; it had all been the evil spirit. The one who lives in my closet.

The next year living in that house was torture for me. Every night, I was scared to sleep in my room. For children, their rooms are supposed to be their sanctuary, where they build worlds of fantasies, but my world was tormented by an evil spirit.

There continued to be odd occurrences in the house like the lights being put on, when Dad had turned them off. Windows open shortly after Mom shut them. The evil bastard in my closet continued his stay, and I continued sobbing about it nightly. For every quirk that happened, there was always an explanation by my parents. Though, they never could provide an explanation for that single and lonely word scrawled into the fog on the window. Bitch.

Years later, my mother would describe an experience that occurred frequently at that home when I was just a baby. When rocking me to sleep at night in the rocking chair, she would often have premonitions. Dreams that would later come true.

On one particular occasion, she was rocking me to sleep when she began to slip into a nap. She claimed she had an intense and alarmingly vivid dream. She stated that the dream began with her rocking me in the rocking chair. As we both fell asleep she dreamed that she was leaving her body. She could see herself sleeping, holding me in the rocking chair that her physical body was actually in. The dream continued and she floated away her body, and up into the night sky.

She then dreamt she was in a car driving with some younger girls she didn't know. In her dream she held the feeling she was in Southern Indiana. The girls were lost. They needed directions. They were lost and panicking and couldn't find anywhere to stop for directions, or to use a payphone.

They finally stopped at a small, creepy cabin near the woods. As they approached the cabin to knock on the door and ask to use a phone, a hideous man opened the door. He was covered in blood and wielding some sort of large knife or axe. My mother could see into the home and there was a bloody, dead, and dismembered woman lying on the cabin floor.

The dream then ended and my mother was awake. I was no longer sleeping in her arms but was fully awake, crying….in my crib.

"How did he get back in his crib?" she asked aloud to herself. "And why is the closet door open?" She shook off the odd feeling surrounding her, and assumed she must have placed me back in while she was dreaming; kind of like sleepwalking. It was the only logical answer.

My mother said that dream was burnt into her memory and for days it was all she could think of. It had felt so real and intense, and she wondered what it meant. Of all dreams, why that?

A few weeks went by, and she forgot about the dream. Until one evening on the nightly news, a story was featured detailing the gruesome murders of some young women. The young women were sexually assaulted, brutally murdered, and dismembered in a cabin near a wooded area in Southern Indiana. According to police, the young women were lost and seeking directions.

When she saw that news, she was first stunned. The dream flooded back into her memory and she just kept staring at the TV. It confirmed her belief that she was shown a psychic premonition or dream. She would often have psychic type premonitions or dreams when rocking me to sleep as an infant.

Months after the writing in the window appeared, my kid sister was born. As an only child, I was very frightened. Scared of the presence inhabiting my closet. Now I had a friend I could play with, and a part of me hoped that together we would be able to defeat the evil spirit. She was such a little thing and I would sit by her all day, guarding her from the unseen forces in that house.

At nighttime, I was jealous of her. She got to sleep with my parents in their room, while I got to stay in my room alone. It was enough having a newborn in their room, and it seemed there wasn't enough room for me.

It wasn't as if they didn't care for me, but the responsibilities of having a new child meant they expected me to grow in some way, and stop with the whole evil spirit story. It also meant they were too occupied to worry about the strange occurrences in the house.

Shortly after my sister was born, my family decided to move. I would find out later when I was much older that my parents decided they couldn't bring up a newborn and their son in such a house. Despite them trying to ignore it, they could feel something wrong in the house. My mom would wake up from nightmares featuring her newborn being drug from her crib, by an unseen force. As her newborn daughter wails for help, she's drug in front of my closet. The door slowly opens, and a dead and rotting arm reaches out, pulling her inside.

In the dream, Mom isn't able to reach her newborn, my sister, in time, and the closet door latches shut. Her infant screams turn to silence as my mother's worst fears come true.

Nightmares like this were frequent. She would awake from these horrid dreams, hurry to her crib and refuse to let go of my sister all through the night. Parallel to the dreams increasing in frequency and

intensity, the odd occurrences accumulated as well. Eventually, they

decided it was time to move.

CHAPTER FOUR

From Frying Pan To Fire?

Our new home was on Cedar Street. A little background: the entire neighborhood had once been inhabited by a Native American tribe, and our new house was built on an Indian burial site. My parents thought we were starting afresh in a new home, free from dramas, but they had no idea what we were walking into.

I was happy with the new home. The first thing I checked when we moved in was my closet. I opened the door and my little self stared in. I didn't think there was a ghost in it. And my theory was propounded at night when I slept peacefully. It was a great feeling for me and my parents. For me, because I wasn't kept scared awake all night. And for my parents because they weren't kept awake by my claims of an evil spirit in my room.

However, my new-found joy faded away in the coming months. I don't know when it started but I began to sense a presence. I would be by myself in the living room watching TV, and I would sense someone watching me from the hallway. It seemed like the person quickly dashed away when I glanced into that direction. I knew it was not my parents. There's something different about a paranormal presence, that makes the hairs on your neck stand. Your ears begin to ring. A sensation envelopes you, making you most uncomfortable. You do not want to be alone. I was always too scared to check it out.

Soon, I noticed that my toys had been moved around. As if someone was playing with them. I would tidy them up and keep them on the shelf, and when I returned they were scattered about. I knew it was not my sister and certainly not my parents.

Somewhere along the way, I started talking with "imaginary friends" (as my mother would call them). My friends, who I had discovered, were the ones who played with my toys when I was not around. Their names were Bobby, Chjules (*pronounced*: *Chew-Layz)*, and Cuhnga (*pronounced: Kong-ah*). Chjules and Cuhnga were Native Americans, and Bobby was a former farmer and owner of the land circa late 1890s.

I knew they weren't like me, but they were my friends and I liked them. When I got back from school, I talked to them about all that had happened in school. My mother would peep through the door and see me talking to myself about how cool the science project had been. In the night, I talked to them before I went to sleep.

This was no one-sided conversation, as I learned from my friends. They were the ones who told me the house had been built on an old burial site. They were the ones who told me about the nearby river and the rituals they used to perform there to appease their gods. They told me a lot of historical facts that I would never have obtained elsewhere.

They told me the *real* facts, and not the altered versions as taught by my history teacher in school. My parents would wonder about how I knew all I did, and I would tell them it was my friends.

I can't recall when exactly my sister, Kortney, got introduced to the trio. Perhaps it was when she grew into a toddler and we started sharing a room. We played with them together, and soon when I wasn't around, she played with them alone.

Our parents probably saw these imaginary friends as a normal phase. Children just being children. It was us being creative. Like most children our age, they thought having imaginary friends was just a phase we would get over.

Like in our previous home, strange events began to happen. One that occurred often was the toilet paper rolls in the bathrooms would be completely unrolled. Kept in neat piles on the bathroom floor, unused.

Whenever my sister and I were asked who unrolled the toilet papers, one or both of us would reply, "It was Bobby!" After all, we had seen him do so.

Voices would be heard throughout the house, as if someone was calling your name. Often though, no one else would be around.

"Yes, Mother, coming!" I shouted back to my mother while rolling my eyes. I was busy doing homework and didn't know why she called for me. I let out an "ugh" and trotted up the stairs to her room. But, she wasn't there. I looked around, went back downstairs, and caught a glimpse of Mom through the front window. She standing near the mailbox and talking with one of the neighbors.

I ran outside and interrupted their conversation. "You called for me, Mom?"

"No, Hun, I didn't. I came out to get the mail when Mrs.-" Mom continued speaking as my mind wondered elsewhere. I knew she had just called for me, I heard it! She was upstairs when she called my name. But how could that be, if she had been outside the whole time?

Looking back, I can assume what it was calling my name that day. And it didn't stop there. Several times I would here my name being called, only to find no one there. Though I never found out exactly who or *what* was calling for me, I certainly know it wasn't my mother.

Our home had a basement. It was very creepy. It was old and damp and was mainly used for storage. The few times I went down with one of my parents, I was always scared. It gave me the chills and I was always glad when we were back up. It reminded me of those nights in our old house with the evil spirit scaring me from the closet.

The door to the cellar-like basement was always kept shut. There was no handrail to grab onto for support, and a few of the boards on the old steps were even loose. Per my parent's instruction, it was to be always kept shut until Dad could get around to fixing it. Several times when they closed the door, they would later find it open. Of course we were the ones they would ask, "Who left the door to the basement open? You know those stairs ain't safe!" One or both of us would reply, "It was Chjules!" or "It was Cuhnga, not me!"

Dad even went as far to install a new latch, doorknob, and other hardware to keep the door from coming open. No matter what he did,

the door refused to stay closed for more than thirty minutes. He would

later come to understand nothing was wrong with the door.

CHAPTER FIVE

Slammin' The Doors

It was a Saturday afternoon. Mom and Kortney had gone for some shopping, and I was home with Dad. I was in my room when I heard the front door unlock, and slam shut. I could hear someone walking around in the kitchen; it was like Mom and Kortney had returned and were placing the grocery bags on the cabinets.

"Mom's home!" I yelled, waking up my dad who was having a nap in his room. I ran to the kitchen to see what they had bought me from the store. I had told them to get me something. Was it a comic book? A video game?

Now get this, there was no one in the kitchen. No one! It was dead quiet. I froze in surprise. I had heard the door open, I had heard someone move around in the kitchen, but now I couldn't see anyone. Dad joined me in a sleepy state.

"Where's your mom?" he asked. I explained what I had heard and he shrugged it off, returning to bed. I brushed it off as my imagination; though, I clearly knew what I had heard.

Late that night, there was a huge noise. The front door slammed with such a force that could be felt through the entire frame of the house. You know there are times when you shut the door to a room, and the windows and walls of that room vibrate? This went through the entire house! It was as if the walls were shaking. It sounded like the door had been pushed off its hinges by a powerful force. That force woke my sister and I from sleep. We literally jumped out of our beds and ran to our parents' room.

Mom was already at the bedroom door. She had probably been on her way to get us. She gestured at us with a whisper into the room, "Come inside the room now!" As she closed the door behind us, I glanced up to see my dad's hands shaking. He was holding his loaded

9mm handgun. This scared me even more than the sound of the

slammed door. My dad barely held that gun. We knew he had one, but it

was safely tucked away, and we didn't know the whereabouts. Him

holding that gun meant this was serious. That we were in danger.

I could hear the fear in his voice as he turned to Mom and said,

"Call the police, someone just broke down our front door!"

Mom gasped as he left the room. I sobbed quietly, I didn't want

him to go out there and confront whoever it was. My mom grabbed the

phone and was trying to call the cops when my father returned. He wore

a dazed look.

"What? What is it?" My mom asked.

"The door is locked and in place," Dad said.

"That can't be!" Mom was stunned.

Together, as a family, we went downstairs. Dad was right. The

door was right in its hinges, and it was locked. We exchanged scared

looks. That force that vibrated through the house had not been our imagination. It had awoken all of us from sleep. Such a sound should have brought the door down. And here it was, the door seeming peaceful like it hadn't been disturbed.

We went back to our rooms. Mom stayed for a while, lingering in the doorway before she left us. As I lay in bed in the aftermath, I was terrified with the silence and stillness. There was something sinister about it, that made me want to hide under the covers. I wasn't alone as my sister kept on tossing around, unable to sleep.

CHAPTER SIX

Late Night Visitor

A few weeks later, we had a late night visitor. I think it was around 2 or 3 am. It was the sound that woke me up. I froze in the bed, my heart racing. The house was so quiet I could hear the footsteps coming up the stairs. Was it Dad or Mom? I knew even then, it wasn't them. There was something odd about the steps. They were extremely lightweight, not making complete contact with the wooden floor.

"Please go away," I kept on saying in my head as the footsteps stopped in front of our room's door. Then it went completely silent for about 30 seconds. Without the door even opening, I felt a presence in the room. The floorboards in our room began to creak softly under the weight of this invisible force.

"Please don't come towards me," I pleaded silently as I lay frozen, afraid to make any move, scared of drawing attention to myself. As if granting my silent prayer, I realized the footsteps weren't headed for me, they were headed towards my sister's bed. So soft were these footsteps, it was as if the presence did not want to awaken her.

Now, I was scared for my sister. As much as I wanted to be a hero and a big brother, I was terrified of the presence. So quickly I didn't first register it, it changed its course and headed towards my side of the room.

I wanted to scream! I wanted to leap out of the bed! But I was so damn scared! I kept on hoping it would suddenly go away. The closet was on my side of the room, and the footsteps were headed that way, the floorboards creaking softly. It was a quiet sound, but I identified it as the closet door being gently opened. The handle slightly turned. I tossed my blanket over my head and quietly asked God to take that thing out of our room. That move must have caught its attention because the footsteps once again changed course; this time towards my bed.

I was shaking. My heart was ready to pop with every step that brought it closer. This is an experience I will never forget because of how terrified I was. Even now when I think of it, I still get the chills.

Then it went quiet. I knew it was standing right by my bed. I could feel its glaring presence, staring at me from the side of the bed. However, the only sound I could hear was that of my parents' snoring down the hall in their bedroom. And then, just as I wondered what it was going to do, I felt the edge of the mattress slightly begin to lower. Whatever was walking around was now sitting on the edge of my bed!

It felt like an eternity. I wanted to jump out of that bed, or scream, but I was too scared of what would happen if I did. The presence knew I was awake, there was no doubt about it; and *it knew*, that *I knew*, it was there. Finally, I felt the presence lift off my bed. I breathed a sigh of relief as it left the room, I could hear the footsteps as it went down the stairs, the same way it had come.

I remained that way, under the blanket, until the hot and stagnant air was too much to bear. What I saw was the only confirmation that what had just happened had not been my imagination. Nor had it been a dream. On the edge of the bed, where that presence had sat was a clear indentation of someone's butt. As well as, indented hand-prints on each side. I had not dreamed it. That presence had been real! It had walked into our room. It had almost gotten into the closet. And it had sat on my bed. That strange presence which scared the hell out of me.

My bladder was suddenly full, with all that transpired; but, instead of going to the toilet, I decided that I would just piss the bed. Better than leaving its comfort and safety. There was just no way I was going to leave my bed or room with that spirit, or whatever it was, probably still downstairs.

CHAPTER SEVEN

Strange Incidents

Years passed and the paranormal activities continued. Family members who visited had one experience or another. They complained of hearing strange footsteps, a presence they couldn't identify, and even someone watching them in a way that made them very uncomfortable. They couldn't stay around long because they were eager to leave and return to normalcy.

One event even frightened the hell out of my Grandmother. She was walking past the basement when she heard a loud "boom". She went down to investigate. To see if we were playing around or if there was a rodent. When she got to the bottom of the stairs, she noticed that a four foot stack of boxes, filled with heavy items, was perfectly flipped upside-down without any damage or spilling of the boxes' contents. She said the basement was very cold, with the hairs on her neck, hands, and legs raised.

She could feel a formidable presence, and she couldn't wait to get away from it. She half-ran upstairs, and it was only then she could breathe calmly again. She didn't want to visit after that incident. Staying over at our home meant one strange incident or another, and the message was passed around family.

Another experience I vividly recall happened when I was in my parents' bedroom. From the corner of my eye, I saw a man's face looking at me through the window.

There was something odd about the man's face; he lacked any defining facial features. His face resembled a photograph whose ink has been smudged and smeared. Even stranger, the window was upstairs on the second floor, with absolutely no balcony, deck, or anything underneath.

I could see him staring at me for what felt like hours, before I gained the courage to fully turn my head and look at him. I was literally shaking.

Who in the hell was this man?! And how in the hell is he floating, peering through the window?! As I turned my head to make eye contact with the man again, he quickly walked away. There was no ground beneath him because he was peering through a second floor window with nothing below it! This was a crazy experience for me. I never told my folks because I didn't want to get into trouble for playing in their room without their knowing.

CHAPTER EIGHT

Do You Know My Name?

The most terrifying incident happened around the time a certain saxophone playing, young, democrat was taking his oath as President of The United States. Recalling this event, has me shaking to this very day.

It was a few weeks after Halloween, and nearing my birthday. I had received an old, and used, Mac computer as a gift; this was one of those ones with giant floppy disks as was in vogue back then. I was so ecstatic, I didn't even mind that my parents decided to put it down in the basement.

One night, when playing games on the computer, I heard footsteps coming down the basement stairs. I had not heard the door open, but I figured I had been too caught up in my game. It was probably Mom telling me it was time to go to bed. I looked up, but I could see no one coming down. The footsteps were getting closer. As the hairs on my arms rose, I already knew what it was.

With each step it took closer down, the light bulb flickered and my heart beat grew faster. I glanced around the room hoping to see Dad or Mom, but no one was there. As the bottom stair let out a slight wooden moan, I panicked and jumped into a pile of laundry sitting nearby on the dusty floor. All this while, I had tried to tell myself that being down here was safe, but I had always known that it was a bad decision. I grabbed some dirty clothing and covered my head, trying to hide and fit into the laundry. I didn't want what I knew was a ghost to see me. I didn't want to have a confrontation with this thing.

There was a bag of Halloween decorations Dad had recently taken down, sitting on the ground in a corner of the basement. My eyes narrowed as it began to move, as if someone was pulling the sack. But I couldn't see any hands or anyone. Then, there was a noise, as made when someone rummages through a grocery bag. Whatever was down there with me was rifling through the bag of Halloween décor, searching for something.

Peeking out from a little corner of the dirty laundry piled on top of me, I watched in horror as the invisible force pulled a creepy, and long nosed, witch mask out of the bag. My eyes popped open as the mask floated towards my hiding spot. It slowly lowered down, close to where I was hiding. The holes in the mask where eyes would normally peer out were completely black. An impenetrable darkness. The mask inched closer to my bunker of soiled clothing.

In the faintest whispers I had ever heard, it asked, "Do you know my name?..."

I was so scared my lips couldn't even open to scream for help. However, it wasn't done with me.

"...Because I know yours," it said in that same cold, faint whisper. Suddenly, the mask fell limply to the ground.

I ran out of the basement as fast as my legs could carry me. I ran smack into my mother who had been on her way to tell me it was time to get to bed. I was breathing so fast there were no words, just sputters. She couldn't understand what I was saying. When I finally calmed down, I tried telling her and my dad what had happened. They went down to the basement, but as expected, whatever had been there was long gone. I knew they believed me. In the past years, we'd had encounter after encounter that left us terrified.

My parents decided shortly after that, it was time to do something about the strange happenings. They began the long and difficult search for someone that could help. After many months, and nearly giving up, they were eventually connected with a local pastor who knew our cries for help were genuine.

They invited the pastor over. The moment he stepped into the house, I saw a look on his face. He said he could clearly feel the presence throughout the home. When we led the pastor into the basement, he immediately concluded it to be the place where the most activity occurs. "This is where it hides," he said referring to a ghost. "Specifically, in that corner," said the pastor while pointing to a small, and unlit, utility room in the basement.

He provided a blessing of the entire home, going room to room praying and sprinkling holy water. He provided my family, especially us children, advice and guidance. The pastor particularly talked to me. Now that I am older, I can't help but wonder if it was because he knew I had more contact (and would continue to have more contact) with these forces than the average person. Or perhaps he could sense we were just a more vulnerable family for these paranormal entities.

He advised us to keep religious text, like The Holy Bible, and spiritual decor on display throughout our house. I remember him telling us never to be afraid. His reason was that often, entities draw power from fear.

"They don't have a physical body, so the only way they can get to you is through fear," he stated. He explained to us what to do if the ghostly entity spoke to us and told us to do harmful, bad things or hurt ourselves.

"Pray for it to leave and then tell your parents who will contact me," he told us.

He also explained the difference between an *intelligent haunt, residual haunt,* and *demonic activity.* It was the first time I got to hear at a young age, that there were different forms of the paranormal. The pastor felt our home was being haunted by an intelligent spirit or maybe even multiple entities.

Before the pastor left, we joined him as a family, with hands held tight in prayer. It was a powerful sight to witness my dad, who at first was skeptical of our home being haunted, pouring out his heart to the Almighty. Asking for God to take this thing out of our home. To protect us in love and peace. It was enough to renew my strength and courage.

We tended not to discuss our experiences with those outside the family, because of the mockery and ridicule. Actually, when my parents were seeking spiritual help, they were told by many churches that their viewpoint on ghosts and the paranormal was that of which "they simply do not exist." Nearly every religious congregation my parents contacted refused to help.

After the pastor performed his work, the paranormal activities lessened. Though, they did not *completely* stop. They became more tolerable, and we became more knowledgeable. As life slowly became more manageable, it also marched on.

CHAPTER NINE

Life Goes On

We moved (only a few miles) to a very rural city, a short while after the pastor's visit. To my relief, and I am sure to my family's, there was no paranormal activity. I remember being on edge when we first moved in, waiting for some presence to show itself. With every sound I heard – footsteps, the wind, creaks – I expected it to be like before. But after a few weeks, I calmed down. I realized we were safe for what seemed to be the first time ever. I couldn't feel that strange tension that usually accompanies haunted homes.

I could sleep with my two eyes closed. I could sleep all night long without being interrupted by some terrifying, unseen force. I could have friends and family come over, since there was no fear of them having an encounter.

The truth is, it was really a huge relief for us all. For over the first decade of my life, the homes we had lived in had been haunted. My folks, who used to think I was just being a kid, had come to realize that there was more; and even if they refused to clearly admit it, they now believed in ghosts and the likes. There had been kind of like a strain, maybe more so - a fear, in the family. We were scared, wondering what was going to happen next. So, for the first time things were going really well. No flickering lights, no breathing down our necks, and no unexplained actions.

I grew up fairly normal at this point, although if you ask my family they would tell you I was a little too rebellious. I would tell you I was a handsome looking kid who melted everyone's heart. As I approached my teenage years, my brother Nick and my sister Brook became the two newest additions to our former family of four.

In high school, I met my fiance, Linds. We were in the same class and started dating my senior year. It was really exciting for me and I was totally in love – I still am. After high school, I moved out of the house into my own one-bedroom apartment in the city. It was a small place, but it was affordable and it was just me; although at this point, Linds was becoming a "live-in".

Three years into our relationship, Linds and I decided to take a big leap – we decided to move in together. We were excited about this decision, this meant we were serious about each other and we had a future together. We had no idea the storm we were about to encounter.

After weeks of searching for an apartment, with no new place to call home, Linds and I finally found a rental house in the historic district of the city. At this point, we were already running out of options. Most of the apartments we had seen were well above our budget, and they certainly didn't resemble their online pictures. However, this rental house (which seemed like our last resort) was within our budget and was very similar to the pictures we had seen. It was a small two-bedroom,

with one bath, atop an unfinished basement. The landlord took us
downstairs to the basement and it felt like Deja Vu; me back in the
basement of my old home. There was a thickness in the air, an almost
visible fog. I brushed it off, dismissing the feeling.

We knew if we didn't get that rental, we might have to let go of
the decision of moving in together. At least until we had enough money
to raise our budget. It seemed like a great little house at the time, and we
paid the rent and moved in.

Moving in was fun. We didn't have much to begin with, but
family and friends helped and even gave us a few items to make it a
home. Having a place of our own made us feel like the adults that we
finally were. It was exciting, until things started happening.

A few weeks in, Linds began to complain about missing items.
This included personal items, and even plates in the kitchen. She would
leave the room for a minute and when she returned her hair brush was
gone. She would search the whole room, going as far as pulling the bed
out, but couldn't find her missing items. It was like a vortex, or some

kind of black hole had swallowed it. And just as she forgot about them

or thought of an explanation for its disappearance, she would find it

somewhere unrelated. The cell phone in the bathroom tub. Her hair

brush in the kitchen sink, or the TV remote in the dirty laundry. She

knew she had in no way moved those items to those places.

Several times, she would join me in the living room, as if I'd

called for her; or, she would call my cell when I wasn't home just to be

clear I wasn't. She felt she was being watched, messed with. She

sometimes heard faint footsteps throughout the house.

The stairs to the basement would ever-so-slightly creak when

she'd be down, working on a pile of laundry. But upon looking up, no

one would ever be there. She could feel eyes on her as she went about

her days. The hairs on her neck would stiffen. She could literally feel

the shadow peeking at her. Whenever she braved an investigation, she

always found no one. But, that stern and heavy thickness was always in

the air. Linds had started to notice this smog more and more often.

"I think the room is stuffy," she would say right before opening a window. But the room, just as the rest of the house, had this invisible fog that clung to it no matter how well ventilated.

And then the scratching sounds started. Though it wasn't loud, you could hear it audibly. Scratching coming from within the walls. Like an animal was stuck and trying to escape. The strange thing was, the sound would seem to follow you from room to room.

When we first heard the scratching, we contacted the landlord thinking it might be a raccoon or similar varmint that decided to take up a nest in the walls. As soon as the landlord would pull in the driveway, the scratching would stop.

We were perfect tenants; quiet, never missed a payment, and provided up-keep on the house. "If it wasn't for that, I wouldn't believe you guys." The landlord once said about the scratching sounds.

I suspected what was going on. It was a routine I was very familiar with. I didn't want to tell Linds what I thought because I felt I would sound crazy. I never told her about my past experiences with the paranormal and how I grew up in haunted homes. Ghosts? Come on! She would certainly NEVER marry me if I told her all that!

During a family gathering, Linds mentioned to my mom the strange occurrences that had been happening in our rental home. Mom froze and stared at me.

"What is it?" Linds asked. She could tell my mom had an idea of what was going on. The rest of the gathering revolved around my mother telling Linds about the haunted homes we had lived in. She gave me a pointed look.

"Nate had his own share. A large chunk I would say."

Linds threw me an unbelievable look that said "seriously, you had an idea what was going on!?" I shrugged in response. Needless to say, Linds was convinced our house was haunted.

One night, we were in the living room watching TV. The door to the creepy basement creaked open. It opened just barely enough to catch our attention. Linds and I locked eyes. It felt like a trip down memory lane. Just as we were processing what was happening, the door slammed shut with a loud bang. My heart raced as what seemed to be a 300lb football player began running down the stairs in such a ruckus. Thud, Thud, Thud; it went down the steps boldly.

Hell no! I hurried to the bedroom and grabbed my pistol and went into the kitchen where I grabbed a large knife and handed it to Linds.

"I am going down there," I said in a small voice I could not recognize. I definitely didn't want to go down there. I would rather eat my own shit, to be honest. But I needed to be the man and defend us. "Get 911," I added.

In a calm voice, which in itself was scary, Linds said, "Why? You and I know there will be nothing down there. At least nothing that we can see. This house is haunted."

I watched her as she went to the kitchen to return the knife. She was right and I was relieved I didn't have to go down there alone.

I didn't know what I would encounter if I did.

The mood was ruined to continue watching TV, or perhaps we just didn't want to be around the basement door. We turned off the TV and cuddled up in the bedroom with the door closed. We laid there quietly, waiting for sleep. What were we going to talk about anyway? The unexplained had just happened, right before our eyes!

As I lay in bed, I realized the paranormal was back in my life. I had truly hoped that aspect was gone for good; that I had said a big *"Fuck You"* to ghosts and all of that creepy, paranormal shit. But here I was, living in a haunted house...again.

CHAPTER TEN

Honey, I'm Home!

Some time later, my coworker, Logan dropped by for a visit. Linds was at work on this particular evening, and wouldn't be home until late. The moment he walked through the door, his face twisted.

"What's wrong?" I asked as I shut the door behind him.

"There's a creepy vibe here, Bro. I don't know how to explain. The air feels thick. Choked up…"

"Welcome to the club", I said silently. I showed him around and I don't know what pushed me, but I took him downstairs to the basement. Perhaps it was just the evil side of me, to see how he was going to react being down there. I didn't know what was going to come out of it.

"Did anyone die here?" He asked in a whisper as his eyes darted around the basement.

"I-"

We both froze. There was a sound from above. The deadbolt on the backdoor was unlocking. Then the sound of the doorknob being twisted. We could hear the door being gently pushed open, followed by the sound of it closing, and the lock being turned back into its place. Then the sound of a few footsteps.

"Linds is home," I said more to myself. I was surprised. She wasn't supposed to get home until much later. "We're down here, Babe!" I called upstairs. I got no reply.

The footsteps moved from the kitchen to the living room, around the house, and then back to the kitchen. We heard the kitchen faucet turn on.

"We should go say hi," Logan said, eager to leave the basement. I hurried after him. As soon as Logan's foot crossed the threshold into the kitchen, he turned to me with a confused look. There was no one there. The water was still running.

"Linds?" I called. Still, no reply. I checked the back door handle, and it was locked. I excused myself and went to the rooms and checked the bath, but Linds wasn't home.

"She isn't here?" Logan asked with an uneasy gulp.

"No, she isn't." I had nothing more to say.

Logan didn't spend any more time in the house. He made up an excuse and left.

He never came back over.

CHAPTER ELEVEN

Seek And You Shall Find

As a young boy, I was scared of the paranormal. As an adult, I was still scared; but, I was also curious. I wanted to know what was causing the incidents. Why were the spirits disturbing our home? Now that I was grown up, I wanted to find answers to these mysteries that had tormented me for most of my life.

As more paranormal activities occurred, I started to do some research. At first, I made use of the internet. Then, it got to a point where I had to supplement by going to the library to find documented history. The first thing I looked into was the history of the land and the history of the house we were renting. The discovery I made was horrifying. You see, in the late 1700s, the land the house sat on was a part of a fort.

Specifically, the section of the fort where Native Americans were held captive.

As I began to reference maps from my city's historical society, I learned a shocking truth which made me nauseous. I overlaid an aerial map printout, with our home clearly visible, against several historical maps. Every time I did this, my home aligned perfectly with the words: *Indian Hanging Grounds.*

Where our home was built, had once been a murder place for Native Americans. It was no wonder why there was such a dark and gloomy atmosphere in the house. Thousands had been held against their will and hung. It sent chills all over my body, and I stared into space. There was certainly no way such cruelty would have happened and the land would have remained the same. Of course, it had to be haunted.

I would have stopped the research at that point, but I began having strange dreams. My nights were haunted with shadows of women and children hanging by their necks. I would approach them in the dream; trying to untie the noose. Trying to help them. But their cold, dead eyes would pop open. Their decaying arms would jerk straight up to my throat. Fingers would wrap around my neck and squeeze into my windpipe with incredible force.

"You'll always end up here," the terrifying, dead, and zombie-like Native American child says; hanging from its noose. Flesh dripping off its bones onto the ground. Chanting in a sadistic song-like manner, "You'll always end up here." Then I would be pulled from the nightmare, to waking life.

The dreams soon changed and featured four bodies, lying dead in a room. The walls and furniture splattered with blood. The scene was a true massacre. The furniture was different, but the room was our living room.

Deep, resonating footsteps begin to pound up the stairs coming from the basement. I knew I must get out, but the dead bodies lie on the ground, blocking the way. As the pounding reaches the top stair, the basement door begins to rattle and I notice the stiff corpses on the floor begin to arrange themselves in a manner to look like an inverted crucifix. The symbol of evil.

I knew it was all connected and I had to research more. I started becoming obsessed with the history of the house we were renting, and the surrounding land. I began spending countless hours trying to find information on the home and property.

During my research, I stumbled across an article that mentioned a horrifying homicide that happened in the neighborhood years ago. I was intrigued and I dug up more articles on. The answers I got were ones I definitely hadn't seen coming.

Four people had been shot to death. They had been murdered unsuspectingly in the living room. The newspaper included several disturbing photographs in its article on the crime.

My eyes widened in disgust and disbelief as I stared at the pictures. One featured the murderer being escorted from the home. One picture showed the living room and a couch speckled with blood. The final snapshot showed the exterior of the home. It was standing tall and menacing. It was the very home Linds and I were living in.

I had to close my eyes and take a deep breath. This shit wasn't real! I opened them and stared at the newspaper. This shit *was* real! The home we were renting was being affected by a dark and evil power, far beyond the average person's understanding. I knew at this point that there was a lot of negative history with the house, a lot of death and evil associated with it.

I continued on with my research and the further I dug into the background of my home, the more the obsession intensified. I was coming up with different truths every time I did research. The house was literally built on the blood and souls of thousands. The more I researched, the more the paranormal occurrences heightened. It was like they were angry, pissed that I was exposing their evil ways.

There were nights we couldn't sleep because of how thick the air was. Nights we lay awake because of the footsteps around the house. It was growing more confident day by day and Linds and I were growing more terrified.

CHAPTER TWELVE

Becoming Possessed

I could feel the surge of energy that was welling in the house, just waiting to explode. I feared what would happen when it did. A lot of unexplained instances happened in the house. People had hurt others without any motive. People had moved out of the house within months of living there. Some had almost gone crazy, while some had not been that fortunate.

I was growing increasingly fascinated (obsessed) with the home, it's history, and the blood-stained land it sat on. My free time was spent investigating every possible piece of information on our home. The obsession slowly began to interfere with my work, as I would spend hours researching. Then it crept into our relationship. I began neglecting the very reason I was in this home in the first place- to be with her. I began to drink alcohol heavily and frequently. Sleep became rare; I stayed up all night searching the internet for answers and drinking booze. I was bordering possession by whatever was inhabiting this home with us, and the alcohol was allowing the supernatural force to break down any mental protection remaining.

Our relationship was strained, and there was a tension between us. We easily got angry with each other, often over the lamest things. Perhaps it was the strain of living with entities, or it was just the power of the entities at work, causing strife between us. I began to wonder if that's always how it started- the strain, moving on to fights, and then bloodshed. We certainly weren't going to wait any longer to find out.

Then it happened. The event that made us realize we were living in a ticking time bomb. I was home alone watching a sports game on TV. Linds was at work. Realizing I was in need of another beer, I made my way to the fridge.

"Shit!" I said as I pulled open the door and glanced inside. "No beer left." And then, a strange thought popped in my head. "Linds hid my beer in the basement," I muttered under my breath. "Sure, Babe, blame all of our problems on my friend, Mr. Bud Weiser." I snickered as I became convinced she was trying to spite me.

Though it made no sense, something was inside my head telling me to go down to the basement to see if there were any brews down there. The normal uneasiness that accompanied thoughts of the basement wasn't there, and I could feel my body being pulled towards the stairs.

Right before my foot hit the last step, I realized I hadn't turned the basement lights on. But, for some strange reason, I didn't care. As I took another step into the pitch-black, musty, and damp basement, I lost my footing and fell to the ground. Before I could pull myself up, I slipped into a dream.

Linds was driving home from a long shift at work when the dread of returning to her "haunted house" weighed over her. "I hope he's not drunk again," she said aloud to herself as she pulled in the driveway. As she was removing her keys from the ignition, she glanced up and noticed how odd the house had looked tonight. Not like it normally was when returning home from work.

Normally, the porch light is on and a bedroom or even the bathroom light could be seen from the driveway. But, not tonight. The house was dark, with no light exiting its windows. She could feel something was terribly wrong.

As she unlocked the backdoor and turned the doorknob, the overwhelmingly thick air from the house rushed out and made her utter a cough. She stepped inside and her stomach turned. The house was silent and in total darkness.

"Where's Nate?" She asked herself. Then she noticed a faint light shining through the crack of the basement door. Fighting fear, she walked over and pushed the door open.

"Babe, you down there?" She called down the stairs. Her heart thumping as she took each step slowly. "Babe?" She called again. As she reached the bottom stair her stomach twisted further in knots. Her heart sank as she saw her lover sitting cross-legged, with only the light of a single candle.

"Why the hell are you sitting down here in the dark?" She managed to ask. She got no response. "What in the hell is going on, you're freaking me out!" She exclaimed.

"Don't be afraid," the words exited my mouth in an unfamiliar accent, with an unfamiliar deepness. My face grew a sickening and contorted smile.

"What have you done with him? Who are you?" Linds asked, fearing the answer she would receive.

"He's fine, for now," the being spoke through my mouth "and as for me- my name is Evil and I am destruction!"

Several hours later I awoke in my bed. My head was throbbing and I felt like I was going to puke. As the blurriness of my vision cleared, I noticed Linds hovering over me.

"Sorry, must have had a few too many beers last night," I said to her, thinking all that had just happened had been a drunken dream.

"Last night?" She asked "Do you mean an hour ago?" I stared at her with confusion.

"You were at work. I had a few beers and was watching the game. I must have passed out and had a crazy dream," I said to her.

"No," She said. "That wasn't a dream. You were possessed."

Looking at her, I noticed the bags under her eyes. How tired she seemed. It was certainly not easy for either of us. We hadn't expected any of this when we decided to move together. A couple would expect issues with cleaning the house, taking out the trash, laundry, cooking dinner and all that. But spiritual entities? Possession? We don't have that in any relationship guides because no one prepares for that.

CHAPTER THIRTEEN

Gone But Not Forgotten

We made the call to the landlord, and informed him that we were moving out. He didn't sound surprised to hear our decision, and I had a feeling the call was one he had expected. I was curious, and wanted to ask him a ton of questions. Had others complained about the house? Had others moved out so quickly? But I held back on those questions. I realized then why such a seemingly good house had been affordable and vacant. No one wanted it. I would rather live in a more expensive place; a place where I had my peace of mind.

A few months later, Linds and I moved out to a small, but beautiful and peaceful, home. The paranormal activities didn't stop before we left. They continued on. But, I think the idea that we were moving soon made us accommodate them. I wished we could have moved out sooner, but searching for a place to live can be very daunting.

I will never forget the day we moved out of that nightmare. The moving truck had already gone ahead, and Linds and I went through the house to make sure we didn't forget anything.

"Want to go downstairs one last time?" Linds asked.

I almost said no, but call it curiosity, I nodded. We went downstairs. It still had that thickness, but it didn't look as creepy as it usually did. However, I was glad when we returned upstairs. Even more glad when we closed the front door, saying our final goodbye. I instantly pitied the next tenants who were going to move in. They certainly had a lot in place for them.

As I drove off, I threw a final look back at the house. God knows I would have almost crashed the car. I don't know what I saw, but I saw *something* in that window; as if watching us go. It sent chills all over my body, just knowing that we were being watched as we left. I told Linds and she was quiet for most of the ride.

"Thank God we are done with it," she finally said.

I totally agreed with her. In the past months, our lives had been tormented by those strange forces, to the point we couldn't have a decent sleep and couldn't even invite visitors over. It was becoming overbearing and uncomfortable. Our home, which was supposed to be our castle, felt like a living hell. Heading back from work or elsewhere, a certain somberness fell on me as I remembered I had to go back to that place which made me so damn uneasy. It is however, an experience that opened my eyes to even more paranormal activities. Prior to this, I had been a young and naive boy.

To this day, I still have nightmares about that house Linds and I rented. In the dream I'm lost, and everywhere I turn, the house pops up. It stands dark and ominous, with that thickness in the air. It invites me in. The porch light turns on, and the door swings wide open. Almost as if welcoming an old friend back home. In my dream I can hear a faint whisper emanating from deep within the walls of the house.

"You may be gone, but you're not forgotten," the voice whispers. I sprint in the opposite direction of the house with my heart pounding in my chest. I can barely breathe from the thickness of the air. As I run, I glance over my shoulder and see a tall, dark figure standing in the doorway.

"No matter where you go, you'll always end up here!" The figure shouts as my legs carry me away. The door slams shut, and then I wake up.

Linds and I have since moved on with our lives, leaving that chapter behind. We've gotten married. We had a child. However, we have *not* forgotten the moment when we realized we weren't alone in that house. We also have not forgotten that the entire world is filled with this same, strange phenomena. And we know it may not be our *last* encounter with these forces.

In one way or another, everyone has experienced paranormal beings. It might be the cool temperature of a room that makes you want to leave immediately. It might be that sense of imminent danger you feel in a place. It could be the feeling of being watched. Pressure on your neck when you sleep. Unexplained injuries. Missing items you can't account for. You might even have a direct, personal encounter with these beings. Whatever your experience has been, I lived through one several times.

CHAPTER FOURTEEN

Living With The Paranormal

At a point in time, you might have no alternative other than accommodating and living with a paranormal being. This might be because of a number of factors. You might have inherited a house; or maybe the rent is so cheap you don't mind having ghosts as roommates. Maybe you are one of those who wants your home rid of them, so you can move on in life. Whatever your story is, I am going to help with some information on how you can live with the paranormal and not get drained. This information has taken years of personal research and experience on my part. I truly hope it proves to be useful.

First, you need to understand that there are a multitude of different forms of spirits. Generally speaking, a typical haunted home is inhabited by one (or even more) of three types of entities.

We have the *residual* and *intelligent spirits*. The residual energy is very common when it comes to house hauntings. It is usually attributed to a traumatic event that took place at a house. This could be murder or suicide; or even something as simple as regular fighting, and intense arguments. This form of haunting does not usually involve a spiritual energy that is *aware* of its surroundings. It is kind of like a playback of past events. The energy could linger in a room or the entire house. Now, some of my old homes had a bit of residual energy. It was why it always felt so creepy, because something horrible happened there.

This energy can affect you. A happy couple may begin to fight in a home where the former tenant was being physically abused by their partner. Children could start being rebellious in a home where a child killed their parents. You get the drift. If the energy is very strong, it can have an effect on its occupants.

How do you know when a dwelling has residual energy? A spot of a room might feel colder than the rest, and you feel more comfortable as you move towards the door. There might be a sudden drop of temperature when you walk in. A thick fog. Feeling certain emotions in a particular room or house; probably fear or anger. It is like a movie playing over and over again. It is energy stuck, repeating the same cycle. This energy is unchanging and cannot be interacted with. It is believed that we leave a bit of residual energy wherever we go, and it often exists in places with lots of energetic build up such as cemeteries, or places where soul loss has occurred. These energies are actually easier to deal with. They can be gotten rid of through a proper house cleansing and blessing.

Intelligent spirit is dynamic. These are the guys you need to worry about. The dude who lived in my closet when I was a little kid was most likely one of these. They can change shape and disappear, and can move from one room of the house to another. If there's a change in the haunting, then you are dealing with an intelligent spirit. These folks can probably hear you when you speak, and they can also communicate with you. Perhaps, through physical objects or through your senses and dreams.

They move things – open doors, make sounds, take items, and can cause havoc. They can be found anywhere. Intelligent spirits can be drawn to residual energy, especially if they have the same background or interest. While these spirits can be gotten rid of, it is certainly not as easy as with residual energy. They tend to mutate overtime; they can become angrier, or calmer.

Intelligent ghosts can be friendly or hostile; they can even be both. Some can reveal themselves to children, as seen with my childhood when I played with imaginary friends. Some tend to hide themselves from adults. Some can hide and remain in the shadows – that was sort of a pun – and you will feel an unexplained presence, but you don't feel threatened.

Then there are the poltergeists. This type of phenomena doesn't hide itself. They want you to know that you are a second tenant, and that they rule the house. They are noisy, they make sounds, turn off lights, play around with objects, and all sort of disturbance. One day you have a ghost playing with the kitchen tap, and the next your home is on fire. Their disturbance may start out slowly, and then intensify.

They can also be very dangerous, living with these guys is not for the fainthearted. They are also stubborn to deal with, and get rid of. They can take more than a clergyman to get them from your home, and they tend to be vengeful. There's one piece of advice when dealing with poltergeist phenomena: Get a professional and be prepared to get out!

Distinguishing the paranormal you are living with will help you determine your next steps. If you realize it is a residual energy, which is fixed in a room, you can have that room properly cleansed and move on. If you have an intelligent ghost which goes about minding its business, even doing a chore or two, then you might as well manage the extra roommate.

And if you have the bad bosses, well, you need to figure out your next steps very carefully, because dealing with the paranormal is not child's play.

-Never Use Ouija Boards or similar objects

I understand the desire for answers, but Ouija boards are not tools you play around with. It might seem like you're fooling around with a "toy", but you have no idea what you may unlock. You may accidentally summon some evil asshole, seeking to torment your poor soul. We don't fully understand the paranormal, and their intentions. Some of them are malevolent and when you make use of these devices, you can unlock more negativity upon yourself and those around you. So, stay away from these devices. They cause you more harm. Don't even use them at drunk parties. Period!

-Don't be afraid to talk about it or ask for help

In the world we live in today, people tend to be religious; but, at the same time, do not believe in supernatural beings. Which, is quite ridiculous. If there's an "Almighty", then why shouldn't you believe in other forms of spirits? Those with supernatural run-ins are often viewed as lunatics. They tell us it is our imagination and they give us an explanation to try and debunk our claims. But we know what we saw. We are not crazy. As we realize how close-minded people are, we tend to keep such experiences to ourselves. No one wants to be judged, teased or frowned upon.

However, that shouldn't stop you from talking about your experiences. It's possible that when growing up, or even as adults, we have experienced some sort of paranormal activity that has us questioning. By talking and sharing with others you will realize that you are not alone. You may also receive some helpful tips (which you should be careful in sieving through. Ghosts are not always the same, remember).

-Recognize the fact that this paranormal thing might not ever go away.

As much as you want it to be, it won't be easy getting rid of a paranormal entity. A cleansing, or even an exorcism, might be done and the paranormal still remains. You might move into a new house and encounter a new paranormal being. Hell, you might even have a paranormal best friend who just wants to tag along with you! You could even hold some psychic powers, drawing these forces to you. So, you have to accept that it might not ever go away. This means you have to embrace the truth.

Accepting this might mean you begin searching for help to remove the entity. Or, learning to "come to terms" with the supernatural; instead of spending countless nights awake in bed. Embracing this knowledge is self-awareness for you. It puts you in a position where you can deal with what is happening with an open mind.

-Educate yourself

An ignorant mind is a foolish mind. You need to educate yourself about your reality. What being is haunting your house? What is the history of your house? Many times, houses and the lands they are built on have gruesome history. It could be the former occupants of the house. Read on all the paranormal materials you come across. Conduct research at the local library. Research reputable sources online. Listen to podcasts. Ask people around town, your neighbors may have information. The oldest person in the neighborhood may have information that can help you.

Educating yourself gives you an advantage to know how best to handle your reality. It also solidifies that you are not crazy. It broadens your mind and makes you open and willing to learn.

Once I got started on educating myself, I learned a lot that made me realize what could be the reason for the lifelong paranormal encounters I have had. This has helped put me on the spiritual path I have chosen today. We are in an era where information is at our fingertips, so make use of it.

-Promote hospitality, positivity and love

Certain beings dwell in negative spaces. Where there is

bitterness, anger and resentment, they thrive. They can take advantage of these emotions and worsen situations, until people physically hurt each other. Some feed on your negative emotions, and you can go further into depression without even realizing it.

I know we all have different lives and we have our own problems, but when dealing with the paranormal you have to be positive. Don't allow anything to bring you down, otherwise you will give up and become a pawn. You need to show love towards all around you. Be hospitable. And be positive. Keep telling yourself the torments will soon be over. Perhaps when they see they have no power over you, they will stop the disturbance.

-Understand that a spirit might have a message

Some spirits have messages to deliver. It could be to a loved one. In some cases it could be to reveal a killer or wrong-doer. They may just need closure before going towards the light. So, they try to get your attention by banging the door, moving around items, etc. Some are just lonely and need someone to acknowledge their presence.

As much as these incidents can be scary, try not to be afraid. Be patient and listen to the message that is being passed across, and your help might just be what the spirit needs to finally rest. These messages can come in dream form, so be on the outlook for them.

-Keep a dream journal

The mind is a powerful force and we don't even fully know what it is capable of. Spirits often use dreams to communicate towards us. This can also help you identify the type of spirit you are dealing with. If you are having recurring dreams where you find yourself in someone's body, then you might be dealing with an intelligent spirit who is able to manipulate forces. By keeping a dream journal, you will spot the patterns in your dream, and you can determine the message the spirit is trying to pass across.

-Pay attention to children and pets

These two are very sensitive to spirits. While adults chalk up imaginary friends and monsters under the bed to creative imagination, children are often able to see these beings in their true forms. We were once children, and as we grow older, we become less sensitive to the glaring truth- that we are not alone.

However, children have a certain innocence that makes them sensitive to the presence of these beings. They are also more in tune with their senses. Hence just as they can easily see spirits, they can also be taken of advantage by demonic forces. So when your child makes observations, don't be quick to dismiss them.

Dogs and cats are very sensitive to the paranormal. I have come across instances of dogs barking at "nothing" or cats hissing at a strange presence crouched in the corner of a dark room. For centuries, animals have been believed to have supernatural influence. Remember the relationship between cats and witches, so it's said they have sight into other worlds. Observe your pets and how they react. They can be a helpful guide when dealing with the unseen.

-Live a normal life

Never allow the paranormal to disrupt your life. You don't want that. You will only end up miserable and depressed. On the outside, I seem like a normal person. I live a simple and normal life. It isn't until someone shows interest before I pour out my knowledge and experience.

Although both worlds exist, it is on different planes. So you need to keep on living your life. Sure, you may live with a ghost. That doesn't mean you can't have a party. Yes, you may have a resident spirit. But that doesn't mean you can't be in a relationship. Don't get *too* wrapped up in the spirit realm, you need to continue living life to the fullest.

-If you feel the paranormal is negative or evil, seek help

Just as they can drain your emotions, demonic spirits can possess and make you do bad things like harming others or yourself. You need to get help if you notice hostility from the paranormal in your home. You will definitely notice the signs if the presence is violent. It is an overbearing presence that can suffocate you and make you want to go mad. Their actions will also help you in determining if they are evil, as well as your research.

Understand that truly evil manifestations often won't make themselves known right away. Those forms of spirits like to work "in the background", usually destroying a persons life through an unseen medium (example: heavy drinking or drugs, violent outbursts, etc).

And also, understand that it might take awhile before you find a qualified person to help. Not everyone out there who says they can help, actually can. Some might be genuine but don't have the *exact* abilities to rid your space of a *specific* ghost or entity. It might take time before you get the right person who will help you in cleansing your home as well as providing valuable information.

These people are usually not everywhere and might not be easy to find. Some tend to live very private lives. You will have to dig deeper. Be patient and you will get the answers you seek.

-Never attempt to remove a paranormal being

This will be dangerous for you if you attempt to remove a demonic spirit or negative presence. Doing so might worsen the situation and intensify its anger, and you or your loved ones might be hurt in the process.

A professional has the experience and knowledge to deal with such a powerful presence, and is in the best position to get rid of the spirit. This could be a priest, a pastor, psychic, shaman, or someone learned in the ways of the paranormal.

For years I experienced paranormal activities, and this shaped my life. These experiences provided me an insight into a world different from the physical world we live in. Ghosts, spirits, and poltergeists seem to be born out of our imaginations; at least we believe so. However, the truth is, we are certainly not alone in this world.

Whether skeptic or believer, everyone experiences strange occurrences that are easily put off because we simply fear the answers. We fear what may be lurking behind the closet door. We fear what may be creeping in the shadows, walking up the stairs. We fear what may be crouched around the corner in the dark basement.

Abandoning that fear, and approaching the supernatural with an open mind is sure to reveal another world. A world separate yet absolutely connected in both past, present, and future. A world filled with mystery and wonder. A world that answers the age-old question of "Where do we go when we die?"

For those currently experiencing the paranormal, I hope you find solace in this book. Though, it may just be a collection of my encounters with the supernatural; I hope you find comfort in knowing, you are not alone in a world surrounded by the paranormal.

BORN

HAUNTED